IVAR THE BONELESS

and the
VIKINGS

DAVID GILL

W

FRANKLIN WATTS
LONDON·SYDNEY

Franklin Watts

First published in Great Britain in 2016
by The Watts Publishing Group

Copyright © The Watts Publishing Group 2016

Series editor: Julia Bird
Series designer: Matt Lilly
Picture researcher: Diana Morris

ISBN 978 1 4451 4715 4

Printed in China

FSC
www.fsc.org
MIX
Paper from
responsible sources
FSC® C104740

Franklin Watts
An imprint of
Hachette Children's Group
Part of The Watts Publishing Group
Carmelite House
50 Victoria Embankment
London EC4Y 0DZ

An Hachette UK Company

www.hachette.co.uk
www.franklinwatts.co.uk

Contents

MEET IVAR THE BONELESS

The fearsome Vikings led wave after wave of attacks on Britain and Europe from the 8th century to the 11th centuries CE. Ivar the Boneless was one of most famous Vikings of all. He headed the largest Viking force ever to attack Britain.

Fearsome Vikings land on a shore, ready to raid.

Who was Ivar?

Ivar the Boneless was the son of a legendary Viking king called Ragnar Lodbrok and his wife, Aslaug. He had several brothers with strange-sounding names such as Sigurd 'Snake-Eye' and Bjorn 'Ironside'.

The Vikings came from the icy lands of Scandinavia.

Where did Ivar live?

Ivar was born somewhere in the countries we now call Scandinavia – Norway, Sweden and Denmark. After he invaded England, Ivar travelled on to Scotland, and then on to Ireland where he lived until his death.

When did Ivar live?

Vikings or 'Norsemen' (men from the north), as they are also known, did not keep written records of births and deaths so it is difficult to know exactly when Ivar was born. He is believed to have first visited Britain in 853. He died suddenly in the year 873.

Why is Ivar famous?

Ivar was a fearsome warrior and a great leader who never lost a battle. His great army came within a whisker of conquering the whole of Britain. If they had succeeded, Britain would have had a very different history.

FASCINATING FACTS

NO ONE REALLY KNOWS HOW OR WHY IVAR GOT HIS UNUSUAL NAME. SEE PAGES 12–13 TO FIND OUT ABOUT SOME THEORIES.

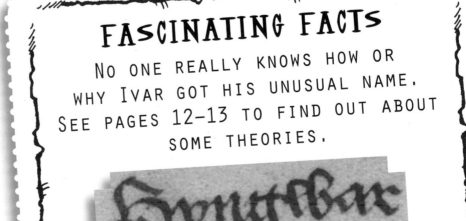

'Hyngwar' – Ivar's name as it appears in an Old English manuscript.

VIKING RAIDERS

The name Viking comes from an old Norse word meaning 'to raid'. At first, the Vikings travelled over the sea from Scandinavia in small raiding parties to steal and plunder, capture and kill. Later they came in their thousands to settle new lands.

The Vikings invaded parts of northern France as well as Britain.

Lindisfarne

One of the first and most famous Viking raids took place at the Christian monastery on the island of Lindisfarne in 793. The Vikings landed swiftly on the isolated, unguarded island, taking the monks by surprise, and launched a savage attack. Buildings were burned, monks murdered or captured and the monastery's many treasures were carried off.

This stone carving shows the Vikings attacking Lindisfarne in 793.

Making Britain home

Viking raids continued up and down the coast of Britain for almost three hundred years. Nowhere was safe. Gradually, however the Vikings stopped raiding and started settling in the north and east of Britain, creating communities and towns. The land and climate in Britain were much more suited to farming than cold, mountainous Scandinavia.

IVAR'S FAMILY

Ivar was born into a famous Viking family. Most of the information we have about Ivar's family comes from Viking sagas. These stories of heroes, battles and mythical creatures are a mix of fact and fantasy.

Ragnar is cast into the deadly pit of vipers.

Ragnar Lodbrok

Ivar's father, Ragnar Lodbrok, is one of the most famous of all the Vikings. His name means 'hairy trousers'. It is said that he was given that name because he once rescued a girl from a huge snake by covering his trousers with tar to protect himself from the snake's venom. He killed the snake and married the girl! In the end, according to the sagas, snakes got their revenge on Ragnar. He was shipwrecked off the coast of England and captured by Aelle, the king of Northumbria. Ragnar was thrown into a pit of vipers and died.

FASCINATING FACTS

RAGNAR RAIDED FRANCE MANY TIMES. IN 845 HE SAILED DOWN THE RIVER SEINE TO ATTACK PARIS. KING CHARLES THE BALD, THE RULER OF FRANCE, GAVE RAGNAR OVER 3,000KG OF SILVER NOT TO DESTROY THE CITY.

Aslaug

As the sagas tell it, Ragnar was fascinated by a young woman called Aslaug, but to test her wits he gave her a riddle to solve. Ragnar told Aslaug to come to him neither dressed nor undressed, neither hungry nor full and neither alone nor in company. Aslaug arrived dressed in a net, with the smell of onion on her breath and with only a dog as a companion. Ragnar was so impressed that he proposed to her. But Aslaug was also wise and she made Ragnar wait a year to test his love for her.

Ragnar and Aslaug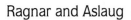

Things to do

In the saga Ragnar gave Aslaug a word puzzle called a riddle to solve.

Try solving these riddles:

What gets wetter and wetter the more it dries?

What can travel all around the world while staying in a corner?

Use reference books or the Internet to check the answers and find more riddles to try out out on your family and friends.

IVAR'S LIFE STORY

Ragnar and Aslaug went on to have many children together, but Ivar remains the most famous.

1 IVAR IS BORN IN SCANDINAVIA, BUT WE DON'T KNOW EXACTLY WHERE OR WHEN.

2

LITTLE IVAR LISTENS TO HIS BRAVE FATHER RAGNAR TELLING STORIES OF HIS TRAVELS AND ADVENTURES.

3

IVAR SETS OFF ON HIS FIRST VIKING RAID.

4 IVAR RECEIVES NEWS THAT HIS FATHER HAS BEEN KILLED.

5 IVAR LANDS IN ENGLAND WITH THE BIGGEST ARMY EVER SEEN.

6

IVAR AND HIS ARMY KILL, PLUNDER AND BURN THEIR WAY ACROSS MUCH OF ENGLAND.

7

THE MERCIAN TRIBE PAY IVAR NOT TO FIGHT THEM.

8

IVAR LEAVES HIS MAIN ARMY TO TRAVEL NORTH TO DUMBARTON, SCOTLAND.

9

IVAR LAYS SIEGE TO THE CITY OF DUMBARTON FOR FOUR MONTHS. EVENTUALLY, HE IS VICTORIOUS.

IF WE CANNOT BREAK IN, WE WILL STARVE THEM OUT.

10

IVAR SELLS PRISONERS AS SLAVES IN DUBLIN, IRELAND.

11

IVAR DIES IN IRELAND FROM SOME KIND OF DISEASE.

12

A SKELETON IS FOUND IN REPTON, DERBYSHIRE IN THE 1970s. SOME BELIEVE IT IS THE BODY OF IVAR.

HE MUST HAVE BEEN A VIKING.

What's in a Name?

The Vikings often gave each other nicknames. Just like today, these names might have had something to do with the way someone looked, their personality or a special gift they had. We do not know why Ivar was called 'the Boneless', but over the years people have suggested many different theories.

Bad bones

Some have suggested that Ivar suffered from brittle bone disease. This condition makes bones weak; they break easily and sufferers can be short. One report describes how Ivar was carried into battle on shields. Was this because he was small? Another claimed that Ivar used a bow rather than a sword. Was this because he was too delicate to fight with his men in the middle of a battle? But would such a man have become the leader of a great Viking army?

Snake-like

In Viking times, snakes were thought to be boneless because of the way they moved, and were believed to be cunning and sly. Ivar was also seen as cunning and sly, which may be why he was compared to a snake. In Viking art dragons often had the face of a snake. Both animals were feared and so too was Ivar.

This Viking grave stone shows a dragon with the face and long tongue of a snake.

A Viking joke

Some things are funny because the opposite is really true. They are called ironic jokes. For example, somebody who is very tall might be called 'Tiny'. Could this have been true of Ivar? Perhaps he was called boneless because in reality he had very long bones which made him much taller than everybody else.

Was Ivar actually tall and strong, like many Viking warriors?

Double-jointed

One writer described Ivar as having cartilage where bones should have been. Cartilage is found in our bodies where bones join together, such as in our knees and fingers, and is flexible and tough. Perhaps the writer meant that Ivar was very flexible in the way he moved, as if he had cartilage where his bones should have been.

What do you think?

Read the evidence carefully and make up your own mind. It does not matter if your opinion is different to someone else who reads this. After all, historians themselves do not always agree.

13

THE GREAT INVASION

In 865 Ivar and two of his brothers set sail for England at the head of a mighty fleet of three to four hundred ships, carrying more than 10,000 men. They were heading for the Kent coast with the sole purpose of bringing England under their control.

Revenge

The invasion was a personal cause for Ivar and his brothers. Their father Ragnar had been killed by the king of Northumbria (see page 8) and they were keen to avenge him. A year after landing in England, Ivar caught up with Aelle and defeated his army. Ivar had Aelle put to death in a most gruesome way.

Vikings often lived along fjords, where there was good farmland and calm waters for their longships (see page 16–17).

Land grab

The second reason for the invasion was more practical. Most of Scandinavia is covered by mountains and the only fertile land is to be found near the coast. By the time Ivar was born much of this was already being farmed. There was just not enough good farmland to go round so Vikings looked to places such as Britain, where they could make a new home for themselves and feed their families.

Use the information below, along with the map, to trace the journey of Ivar's army.

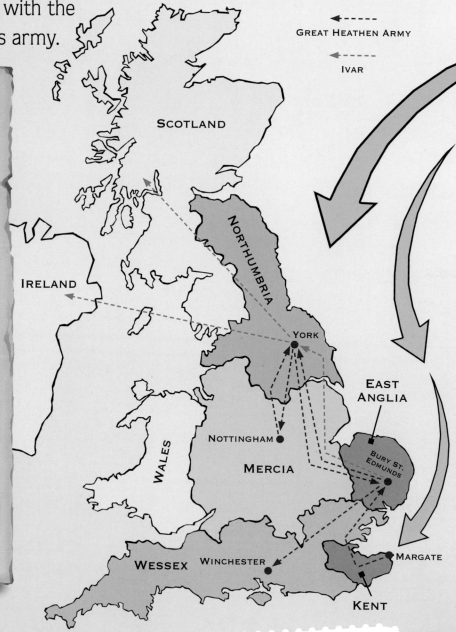

GREAT HEATHEN ARMY

IVAR

SCOTLAND

NORTHUMBRIA

IRELAND

YORK

EAST ANGLIA

WALES

NOTTINGHAM

MERCIA

BURY ST. EDMUNDS

WESSEX WINCHESTER

MARGATE

KENT

1. In 865 a huge fleet of Viking ships led by Ivar land on the coast of Kent.

2. The Viking army marches to Bury St Edmunds in East Anglia to spend the winter there. Ivar forces Edmund, the king of East Anglia, to pay him for not destroying Edmund's land.

3. In 866 the Vikings march to York in Northumbria. They win a great battle and are now in charge there.

4. In 868 Vikings march south to Nottingham. Burghred, the king of Mercia, asks the people of Wessex for help. In the end, Burghred makes a deal and pays Ivar to leave his land.

5. The Vikings go back to York in Northumbria.

6. In 869 the Vikings march back to East Anglia. They kill King Edmund and take control of his kingdom.

7. In 870 Ivar leaves the main army and returns to Northumbria. From there, he travels on to Scotland and Ireland.

8. The main Viking army marches on to Winchester in Wessex, the only kingdom left for the Vikings to conquer.

FASCINATING FACTS

Bury St Edmunds is a town in Suffolk, England. It is named after King Edmund of East Anglia, who was brutally murdered by Ivar's men. They tied him to a tree and used him as target practice for their arrows. Soon after he died, Edmund was made a saint by the Pope, the head of the Roman Catholic Church.

VIKINGS RULE THE WAVES

Ivar and his army travelled to the islands of Britain on longships. Vikings were great craftsmen and excelled at building ships. Their longships became the perfect vehicle for Viking raiders.

The Gokstad longship was dug up by archaeologists in Norway in 1879. The boat dates back to 850 so it would have sailed the seas at the time of Ivar the Boneless.

Water warriors

Longships came in all sizes. They might be as big as thirty metres long and carry fifty to sixty men or just ten metres long with a crew of ten men. Longships all had the same basic shape though, and they were made in the same way, with overlapping planks of oak nailed together and tarred hair stuffed in the gaps to make them watertight. Longships were powered by one large sail and a crew of

Viking longships sail the seas

Viking oarsmen. They were long, sleek, fast, easy to handle, stable in high seas and shallow enough for sailing up rivers. This allowed Vikings raiders to sail stealthily up rivers and ambush their unlucky victims on the nearby shore.

Ships of death

A dragon or serpent's head was often fixed to the bow (front) of a Viking longship. These creatures represent fear and death and that is just what Vikings wanted their enemies to think was heading their way. Ivar the Boneless had a raven printed on the sail of his longboat. In Viking stories ravens were always present at a battle, flying low over the dead and the dying.

The bow of this Viking longship is decorated with a dragon's head.

Finding the way

Ravens were also used to help the Vikings navigate across the open seas. Floki Vilgerõarson, a Viking explorer who lived at the same time as Ivar, would release a raven when he thought land should be near. If it circled the boat land was not near, but if it took off in a certain direction the boat followed.

Things to do

Try making your own model of a Viking longboat. Here is a good template to follow:

http://downloads.bbc.co.uk/ history/handsonhistory/ vikings_longship.pdf

THE FIGHT FOR BRITAIN

Ivar and his men spent five years battling the kingdoms of England. In 870, as they were about to invade the last surviving kingdom, Wessex, Ivar left to journey north to Scotland.

Ivar in Scotland

In 871 Ivar and his men reached Dumbarton, then the capital of that part of Scotland. The town was well defended with a large wooden palisade (fence) that went around the town. Ivar cut off the food and water supply to the town and laid siege to its inhabitants. He waited for almost four long months before the people gave in. His men destroyed the buildings and took many people away to be sold as slaves.

The Vikings, led by Ivar, land to lay siege to the walled town of Dumbarton.

HISTORY LINKS

ALL THROUGH HISTORY, SIEGES HAVE BEEN A COMMON WAY OF TRYING TO DEFEAT AN ENEMY. THE MOST BESIEGED CITY IN HISTORY IS JERUSALEM, AN ANCIENT CITY IN ISRAEL. IT HAS BEEN BESIEGED 27 TIMES. JERUSALEM IS SPECIAL TO JEWS, MUSLIMS AND CHRISTIANS AND THEY HAVE ALL WANTED TO CONTROL IT AT DIFFERENT TIMES THROUGH HISTORY.

Jerusalem, the most besieged city in history.

Ivar in Ireland

From Scotland, Ivar journeyed onto Ireland. He had landed in Ireland around 12 years before he invaded England. He and fellow Viking Olaf the White settled in a place which later became known as Dublin – now the capital of Ireland. When Ivar returned to Dublin in 871 he brought with him hundreds of English and Scottish prisoners. They were very valuable to Ivar as he could sell them as slaves. Some were taken to other countries and sold in the slave markets there.

A Viking sells a girl slave to a Persian merchant.

Wessex resists

While Ivar and his men took control of Ireland, the remains of the Great Heathen Army were losing ground in England. After numerous battles with the army of the kingdom of Wessex, led by King Alfred the Great, eventually the Vikings were defeated in May 878. A peace was agreed and the Viking leader Guthrum converted to Christianity.

Things to do: Viking place names

Using a map of Britain, look for place names that end with: __by __kirk __loft __thwaite __thorpe or __throp. These places will usually have been Viking villages or towns.

The website http://jorvik-viking-centre.co.uk will give you information to help you in your research.

VIKING BELIEFS

Ivar was a pagan, like most Vikings. They believed in many different gods, rather than one main one. The Vikings prayed to these gods for their help and protection. In the years after Ivar died, more and more Vikings in Britain converted to Christianity.

Things to do

Find out more about these Viking gods:

Thor, Odin, Frey, Freya, Loki and Hel.

Thor

Freya

An engraving of the mythical Viking tree Yggdrasil

Worlds apart

The Vikings believed that the world was divided into different kingdoms. At the top, there was a sky kingdom called Asgard where the gods lived. In the middle was Midgard, the home of people. It was connected to Asgard by a rainbow bridge. Deep below the Earth was Helheim, the home of the dead. In between these three kingdoms were various other realms, inhabited by magical creatures such as giants, dwarves and elves. Holding all these worlds together was a gigantic tree with magical powers named Yggdrasil.

A warrior's death

Like many Viking warriors, Ivar wore a hammer pendant around his neck. This was a symbol of the great god Thor, who carried a mighty hammer called Mjollnir. The Vikings believed that wearing the pendant would bring them luck in battle. All Viking fighters preferred to die a hero's death in battle. If they did, ghosts of female warriors called Valkyries, who flew on horses over every battlefield, would swoop down and take them to Valhalla, the Great Hall in Asgard. Unfortunately, Ivar is believed to have died of a disease so, according to Viking law, he would have ended up in Helheim.

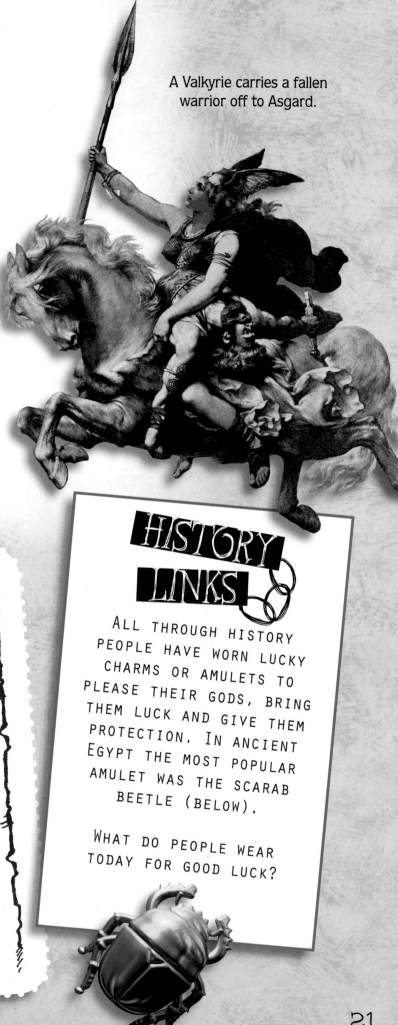

A Valkyrie carries a fallen warrior off to Asgard.

FASCINATING FACTS

THREE DAYS OF OUR WEEK ARE NAMED AFTER VIKING GODS:

WEDNESDAY IS NAMED AFTER ODIN. THE NORSE WORD FOR ODIN IS 'WODEN' (WODEN'S DAY)

THURSDAY IS NAMED AFTER THOR, GOD OF THUNDER (THOR'S DAY)

FRIDAY IS NAMED AFTER FREYA, GODDESS OF LOVE AND BEAUTY (FREYA'S DAY)

HISTORY LINKS

ALL THROUGH HISTORY PEOPLE HAVE WORN LUCKY CHARMS OR AMULETS TO PLEASE THEIR GODS, BRING THEM LUCK AND GIVE THEM PROTECTION. IN ANCIENT EGYPT THE MOST POPULAR AMULET WAS THE SCARAB BEETLE (BELOW).

WHAT DO PEOPLE WEAR TODAY FOR GOOD LUCK?

A Viking Creation Story

Different peoples around the world have their own stories of how our world was formed. Here is a Viking story about the creation of the world they saw around them. It is a story Ivar would have known well.

In the beginning, before anything existed, there was a huge emptiness. No light, no darkness, no sound, just a vast, empty space which the Vikings called Ginnungagap.

No-one knew the secret of how the first land was created but everyone knew it was formed in two parts, the land of fire and the land of ice.

Deep within the Earth lay a simmering lake of fire where there lived a demon called Surt. He guarded the land of fire, called Muspelheim, with his sword, forged in the lake's fiery furnace. Surt spat out great globs of red hot lava through the cracks in the Earth's shell. Rivers of lava flowed down mountains, scorching, scalding, blistering, burning everything in its path. When the lava cooled it turned into a thick layer of volcanic dust that covered the Earth.

In the land of ice, Nilfheim, huge mountains of icy rock erupted out of snowfields that stretched endlessly in every direction. Winds howled across the glaciers, hail fell like bullets, freezing rain turned to daggers of ice. The biting cold turned the Earth into a white wilderness.

Bit by bit the land of fire and the land of ice grew and spread until at last the two lands came together. Their collision caused a violent, awesome explosion. Water and dust erupted high into the air, swirling, dancing together until they combined to form a giant, who became known to all as 'Ymir'. From out of the giant's armpit was born a male and then a female. Ymir also gave life to a six-headed son, the first of the mountain giants.

Creation had given birth to giants and gods, men and women, but they did not live in peace with each other. The waters of the sea had been poisoned and their poison polluted the minds of many. There was anger, there was jealousy, there was pride and there was war!

In the fighting between giants and gods, Ymir, the first to breathe the air of life, was killed. His body was used to create the Earth. His blood made the oceans, seas and rivers. Teeth were transformed into rocks, bones were ground into powder that filled the desert and beaches. Hair was used to make the trees and bushes and the wings of eagles beat the air to form the wind. The sky was held in place by dwarves and the Earth was separated into the land of men and the land of gods such as Odin, Thor and Freya.

Things to do: creative writing

In this creation story the body of Ymir was used to make oceans, desert and trees. Try writing your own story behind the creation of any of these:

The Sun, the Moon, stars, lightning, thunder, volcano, earthquakes.

THE END OF IVAR

Ivar is believed to have died suddenly in Ireland in 873. However, like much else in Ivar's life, the details are unclear and historians still disagree about what happened to him.

Ivar's death and burial

People who recorded the history of Ireland wrote that Ivar died of a terrible disease and was buried there. But the saga of Ragnar Lodbrok claims Ivar was buried in England. Some archaeologists believe that the skeleton of a body found buried in a churchyard in Repton, Derbyshire, along with a Thor's hammer pendant and a sword, is the body of Ivar the Boneless. The Vikings were known to spend winter there and the skeleton was surrounded by many other Viking skeletons, indicating he had been an important person. The man died a violent death with blows to the head, arm and thigh. Could this really be Ivar? If so, he did not die from a disease.

The replica Thor's hammer that was found with the mysterious Viking skeleton

The reconstruction of a Viking head found at Repton. Could this be the face of Ivar?

The early settlement of Dublin

Ivar's legacy

In the end, Ivar failed in his quest to defeat the Anglo-Saxon people, conquer Britain and turn it into a Viking kingdom. He very nearly succeeded and perhaps if Ivar had stayed with all of his army he might have defeated Alfred the Great (see page 19). If that had happened the history of Britain would have been very different.

However, Ivar richly deserves his place amongst the great Viking figures. He and his friend Olaf the White founded the city of Dublin, now the capital of Ireland. Ivar also led the biggest Viking invasion force ever to hit the shores of Britain and it is said that he never lost a battle. That alone is a great achievement.

IVAR WAS NOT THE ONLY BRITISH LEADER WHOSE DEATH WE ARE UNSURE ABOUT. ON THE NIGHT OF 21 SEPTEMBER 1327 EDWARD II WAS MURDERED ON THE ORDERS OF HIS WIFE AND HER LOVER. BUT WAS HE? SOME HISTORIANS BELIEVE EDWARD ESCAPED TO ITALY VIA CORK, IN IRELAND.

HOW DO WE KNOW?

Trying to find out about Ivar is like making a jigsaw picture when we do not have all the pieces. Even though we do not know everything about Ivar, we can still see what he may have been like from the pieces of information we have about him.

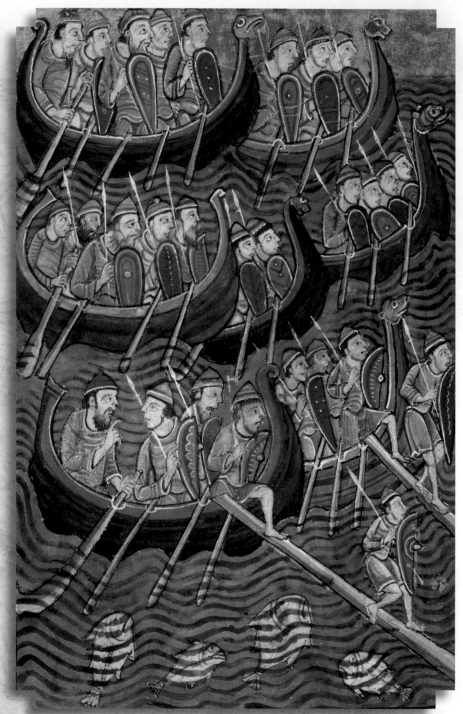

A medieval painting that shows the Great Heathen Army heading towards Britain.

Written sources

Ivar is mentioned in many different writings, though most of these only give us tiny bits of information. His name is recorded in the *Anglo-Saxon Chronicles* as the leader of the Great Heathen Army which invaded England in 865. Some of his story is told in biographies of famous people such as Alfred the Great and in the history of places like Dublin. We can also read about Ivar's adventures in Viking sagas, but these are a mixture of fact and fiction. To find out what Ivar was like we sometimes have to pick out what is real in these stories from what is made up.

FASCINATING FACTS

LIKE SOME OTHER VIKING WARRIORS, IVAR WAS SAID TO BE A BERSERKER — SOMEONE WHO WENT INTO A MAD FRENZY BEFORE GOING INTO BATTLE. IT WAS A WAY OF BUILDING COURAGE AND TERRIFYING THE ENEMY. THIS IS WHERE WE GET OUR MODERN EXPRESSION 'TO GO BERSERK'!

What was Ivar like?

We can sometimes make up our minds about what somebody is like by examining things they did. Look at these key facts about Ivar and make up your own mind about what kind of man he was.

When Ivar came to England, he sought out and captured the man who had killed his father. Ivar then had him killed in a most horrible way.

Ivar attacked the city of York on *All Saints' Day* when he knew people would be busy celebrating a religious festival.

When Ivar saw the size of his enemy's army at Nottingham he thought he might not win the battle so he persuaded them to agree to a peace treaty. His enemy ended up paying Ivar silver and gold not to fight them.

What do you think?

One writer said Ivar was a fearless warrior who was always at the front of the fighting. Another writer said Ivar's favourite weapon was a bow, but they are used some distance away from the fighting.

Can both writers be right?

What do you think?

VIKING EXPLORERS

In the years around and after Ivar's death, the Vikings voyaged further and further around the world, reaching Asia in the east and the coast of America in the west.

Vikings took to the water to sell and buy goods, as well as to trade.

Eastern trade

The Vikings were well-known as raiders, but they were also traders who constantly looked for places where they could sell and buy goods. While Ivar was leading the invasion of Britain, Vikings living in Sweden travelled east along the Baltic Sea and along rivers in what is now part of Russia. Some reached settlements such as Baghdad in modern-day Iraq. Others landed at the great trading city of Constantinople (now Istanbul). On their travels, they traded goods from their homelands such as furs, amber and slaves for silk, spices and pottery, among many other things.

Westward Ho!

Vikings living in Norway sailed west. Some made the short journey to the Shetland Isles and the Orkneys off the coast of Scotland. In the 9th century, they sailed further west and discovered Iceland. Later, Viking explorer Erik the Red sailed even further and found Greenland. Around the year 1000 Erik's son, Leif Erikson, sailed the furthest west yet and became the first European to set foot in America.

A statue of Leif Erikson

IVAR'S BROTHER BJORN IRONSIDE WAS BUSY RAIDING THE COASTS OF SPAIN AND NORTH AFRICA DURING IVAR'S INVASION. AS HE WAS MAKING HIS WAY HOME, A SARACEN (MUSLIM) FLEET CAUGHT UP WITH HIM AND LAUNCHED A TERRIFYING WEAPON CALLED 'GREEK FIRE'. ALTHOUGH BJORN LOST FORTY SHIPS, HE DID ESCAPE AND RETURNED TO NORWAY.

Greek Fire could burn even on the surface of the sea.

End of the Viking age

Vikings continued to play an important role in Britain up until the Norman invasion. In September 1066 Harald Hardrada, the Viking king of Norway, landed near Newcastle with three hundred ships, determined to take the English crown. He was defeated by King Harold II of England at the Battle of Stamford Bridge. King Harold then had to march over 400 km south with his weary troops to face William of Normandy at the Battle of Hastings. Hardrada's attempted invasion probably cost Harold victory and led to England being ruled by the Normans for the next hundred years.

My Own Research

Use an atlas to trace the journeys of Bjorn Ironside and Erik the Red and his son.

Where might Leif Erikson have landed in America?

Timeline

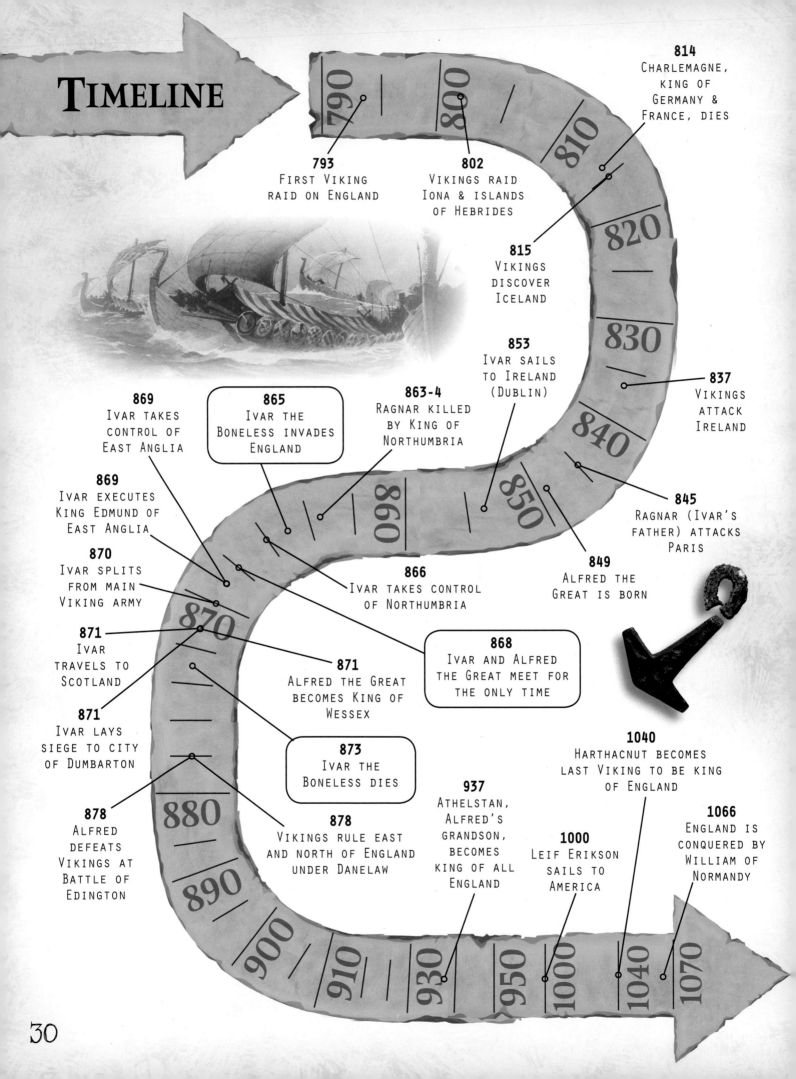

793
First Viking raid on England

802
Vikings raid Iona & islands of Hebrides

814
Charlemagne, king of Germany & France, dies

815
Vikings discover Iceland

837
Vikings attack Ireland

845
Ragnar (Ivar's father) attacks Paris

853
Ivar sails to Ireland (Dublin)

849
Alfred the Great is born

863-4
Ragnar killed by King of Northumbria

865
Ivar the Boneless invades England

869
Ivar takes control of East Anglia

869
Ivar executes King Edmund of East Anglia

870
Ivar splits from main Viking army

866
Ivar takes control of Northumbria

868
Ivar and Alfred the Great meet for the only time

871
Ivar travels to Scotland

871
Ivar lays siege to city of Dumbarton

871
Alfred the Great becomes King of Wessex

873
Ivar the Boneless dies

878
Alfred defeats Vikings at Battle of Edington

878
Vikings rule east and north of England under Danelaw

937
Athelstan, Alfred's grandson, becomes king of all England

1000
Leif Erikson sails to America

1040
Harthacnut becomes last Viking to be king of England

1066
England is conquered by William of Normandy

30

GLOSSARY

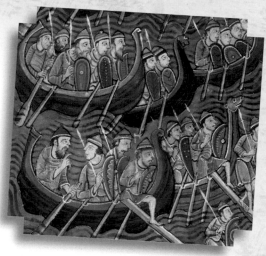

Amber a hard yellow-brown substance that can be used to make jewellery

Anglo-Saxons northern European tribes that settled in Britain from the 5th century

Ancestors the people from who you are descended

Conquer to take over a place by force

Fertile rich; good for growing plants in

Heathen someone who doesn't follow any religion

Ides the 15th day of March, May, July and October and the 13th day of other months

Monastery a place where monks live

Pagan a person who does not follow one of the six main faiths

Saga Viking tales that were often a blend of fact and fantasy

Siege when an army surrounds a place and cuts off its supplies in order to force out its inhabitants

Slaves people who are considered to be owned by others and are forced to work for no pay

THE GREAT IVAR THE BONELESS QUIZ

1. What was the name of Ivar's father?

2. In what year did Ivar invade England as leader of a great Viking army?

3. What name was used to describe the Vikings in the *Anglo-Saxon Chronicles*?

4. Which Irish city was founded by Ivar and his friend Olaf?

5. What did Ivar wear around his neck?

6. What is the place where Viking warriors believed they went to if they died in battle?

7. Which Viking sailed all the way to America five hundred years before Christopher Columbus?

8. What was the name of the mythical Viking tree?

9. Which creature was often carved on the bow of a Viking longship?

10. Which was the only Anglo-Saxon kingdom not to be conquered by the Vikings?

Answers on page 32

31

INDEX

QUIZ ANSWERS

1. Ragnar Lodbrok **2.** 865 **3.** Danes **4.** Dublin **5.** Hammer of Thor
6. Valhalla **7.** Leif Erikson **8.** Yggdrasil
9. Dragon or serpent **10.** Wessex